FOREWORD
By Dr. Marion Nelson

Vesterheim: The Norwegian American M

Vesterheim means "western home" and was the word used by Norwegian immigrants in referring to their home in the New World. It is also the name of the Norwegian-American Museum at Decorah, Iowa. For an institution devoted to preserving the culture brought by the Norwegians to America, the name is appropriate.

Founded in 1877, Vesterheim is the oldest and most comprehensive immigrant ethnic museum in the country. Its location in Decorah, Iowa, is the result of historic circumstance. It was here in 1850 that the Norwegians of the upper midwest established their first large and lasting settlement west of the Mississippi. For several decades Decorah served as a gateway to Norwegian expansion north and west. Located between the old settlements in Wisconsin and the new frontier, Decorah became the home of a leading immigrant newspaper, *Decorah Posten*, and of the first Norwegian-American degree-granting institution, Luther College. It was at Luther that the Museum was begun. Historic circumstance could not have done better. Decorah is in a wooded valley reminiscent of the landscape from which many immigrants came.

The history of Vesterheim is marked by three stages of exceptional growth. The first occurred around 1900 when Haldor Hanson, a musician by profession, was curator. Although the collection at that time served primarily college purposes, Hanson recognized the importance of collecting material relating to the group by whom the College was founded. Simple objects for everyday use as well as distinctively decorated pieces from

Norwegian immigrant homes were acquired for the collection, and a project to preserve all the Norwegian periodicals and newspapers published in America got underway.

The second period of exceptional growth came during the 1920's and 1930's when the leading figure was Knut Gjerset, a Professor of History at Luther College. His major contribution was in acquisitions. In 1925 he negotiated a massive gift of duplicate materials from museums in Norway. Several large shipments were sent between 1927 and 1939. In 1930 he purchased for the Museum the private collection of P.D. Peterson, Eau Claire, Wisconsin, a collection which had in itself constituted a mini-museum in the Eau Claire Public Library. Also in 1930, Gjerset added three immigrant buildings to the outdoor division. It had been established in 1913 as an innovation in American museum practice when the building which housed the first Norwegian pastor to settle west of the Mississippi was moved to the college grounds for preservation. In addition to these major efforts, Gjerset continued his search for important immigrant materials in private homes. His major acquisition occurred in 1932 when he acquired the historic Lutheran Publishing Company building (previously the Arlington House) in downtown Decorah as a home for the collection. It is still the main building in the Vesterheim complex.

The Museum's most recent phase of expansion began in 1964 when a non-profit corporation was founded to assume responsibility for the collection and to develop a program for its preservation, growth, and utilization for educational purposes. It

The main building of Vesterheim, a restored hotel from 1877, with additional historic buildings of the Museum complex in the background.

1

was under the new corporation that the name Vesterheim was adopted and Marion Nelson, Professor of Art History at the University of Minnesota, was hired as Director. He still retains this position after twenty years during which the staff has grown to twelve employees and the size of the collection has almost doubled.

Three major achievements during this recent phase of growth are having acquired and/or renovated 36,000 square feet of floor space in historic buildings to house the Museum's collections and service units, having organized the collection into interpretive exhibits, and having established an aggressive program in the preservation and promotion of traditional Norwegian crafts.

Vesterheim is now an institution of over 6,000 members from all parts of the United States and many foreign countries with a training program in traditional crafts which serves approximately 350 students annually. Although located in a city of less than 8,000 inhabitants, its annual visitation is three times that number.

The material in the Museum collections represents the life and culture of the immigrants before leaving Norway and after arriving in the New World. The folk museum idea, which originated in late nineteenth century Scandinavia and emphasizes total cultures rather than only an elite, is prominent in the Museum's planning. Vesterheim's collecting policy stresses the common man in both his outdoor and indoor environments.

The range of materials preserved at Vesterheim is great. Highest priority is given to objects produced by Americans of Norwegian heritage which still reflect the ethnic background of the maker. These include the simple implements of farm and home as well as works of art created for edification or pleasure. Of almost equal significance are materials brought from Norway to serve the immigrant's needs while crossing the Atlantic and getting established in the New World. All objects which played a role in the transition of the immigrant from his old world existence to life as an American have some place at Vesterheim. The collection is designed to allow Americans of Norwegian stock to experience their cultural history through the actual materials of which that history was made. It is also designed to show other Americans which threads in the fabric of the New World go back to Norway.

Vesterheim Center, a restored industrial block from the 1860's, in which the museum's classrooms and other service units are located.

The Stone Mill and Blacksmith Shop, both from the 1850's, which make up the Industrial Division of Vesterheim.

Darrell Henning, Curator at Vesterheim, demonstrates smithing in the Museum's blacksmith shop.

A trunk from Hallingdal in the Vesterheim collection.

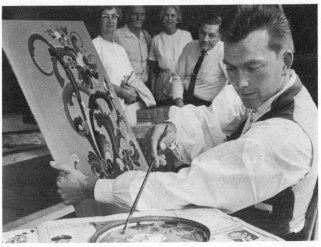

Sigmund Aarseth of Valdres, Norway, the first painter brought from abroad to demonstrate and teach rosemaling at Vesterheim, astonishes visitors at the Decorah Nordic Fest in 1967 with his facile technique and spontaneous style.

Hans Wold of Modum, Norway, demonstrates to students at Vesterheim that even fingers can be used for rosemaling.

The Valdres House, a residence built around 1800 in Valdres, Norway, and moved to the outdoor Division of Vesterheim in the early 1970's.

Rosemaling: its origins and development

Rosemaling was the final flourish of a long folk art tradition in Norway. That tradition had roots going back to the Viking period; but until the 18th century, it did not include much painting. Weaving and woodcarving were the major media through which the artistic impulses of the Norwegian people in the early days found expression. When open hearths gave way to corner fireplaces with chimneys in the 18th century, the old art of decorative painting, which since the Middle Ages had been prominent in churches and the homes of merchants, industrialists, and government officials, also found its way into farm interiors.

Getting rid of the soot from open hearths was not the only change in the 1700's which prepared the way for decorative painting in rural Norway. Glass was now also becoming more available, which meant that windows along the walls could replace the small smoke hole in the ceiling as the source of light. With windows, the interior for the first time became bright enough for colors to be adequately seen. At the time of this revolution in lighting, water powered sawmills also appeared in the inner valleys producing boards for making panelled furniture and for covering walls and ceilings. Their smooth surfaces were more suited to paint than were those of the hand-hewn planks and logs that had preceded them.

Into the well-lit, soot-free, and often panelled new interior, paint makes a dramatic entry. Walls, furniture, and household containers now become the objects of an attack with paint which came to characterize Norwegian folk art of the 19th century. The major motifs in this decorative revolution were floral scrolls in brilliantly contrasting primary colors. The spiralling and intertwining forms of animal carving in the Viking Age and acanthus carving of a period just preceding rosemaling now return in the swirling vines of the new art.

To call the painted scrolls that acquire such prominence in the homes of Telemark, Hallingdal, and other regions in Norway around 1800 "new" is not quite accurate. The painters who created them had seen the work of master decorators in churches or middle and upper class homes. These artists of urban training had brought the Baroque and Rococo styles of continental Europe into the deep valleys of Norway. The styles were also disseminated through prints and the decoration on the cast panels for iron stoves, the production of which was a major industry in 18th century Norway.

Rosemaling is a product of the meeting between outside influences and deep-rooted local traditions, the latter having developed primarily in textiles and carving. The materials and techniques of rosemaling were largely those of the city painters, with the oil and most of the pigments coming from abroad. The local characteristics which were added to the essentially European design elements were the tendencies toward complex and often interlacing designs and the use of primary colors.

Economic circumstances also contributed to the rise of rosemaling. The combination of an improving economy and of a rapidly increasing population led to an accumulation of wealth for the larger landowners but also to an increasing number of cotters, small landowners, and day laborers whose circumstances were more and more deprived. The land could not support the numbers it was producing, and industry in Norway was not ready to absorb the overflow.

Most of the early rosemalers whose history is known came from the deprived group. For many, painting was a necessary

A conservator at Vesterheim cleans the surface of a trunk from 1860 in the Museum collection.

source of income. The artists had ready patrons in the families on larger farms whose circumstances had improved and who more and more were patterning their lives on those of the upper classes. The homes of the merchants, the officers, and the industrialists at this time had walls, furniture, and small objects that were generally covered with floral decorations in the Baroque and Rococo styles. The country painters who became the decorators for the nouveau riche of the rural population received little more than their keep for their work, but this meant one less mouth to feed from the limited produce of their small farms or cotter's fields. Rosemaling was an art developed among the poor to make a living while satisfying the tastes of the more fortunate.

With the beginning of mass emigration in the 1840's and 50's, many farmers who had developed the art of decorative painting headed west to seek a better livelihood in the New World. There, where open fields were available for little cost and manual labor gave better return than painting, art work was almost immediately abandoned. Very few of the early immigrant artists appear ever to have picked up brushes again. The examples of early rosemaling done in this country can be counted on one's fingers while records show that many of the established rural painters left Norway for America.

By the 1930's, the immigrants began to recognize their cultural loss. Per Lysne, an experienced painter who had come to Stoughton, Wisconsin, during the second great wave of emigration shortly after 1900, returned full time to decorating in the Norwegian style during the Depression. The old styles of painting, vaguely remembered from immigrant trunks, struck a familiar chord to members of the immigrant community when

they reappeared in Lysne's work. In spite of the depressed economy, he had no problem selling his decorated furniture and smaller pieces or in getting commissions for larger decorative schemes. Although rosemaling had been a man's art in Norway, it was now women in particular who recognized the charm and beauty of this style from their half-forgotten past. It appealed in itself and it gave immigrant women something to identify themselves with in the gray mass of the melting pot.

Rosemaling as a community phenomenon in America developed first in the areas surrounding Stoughton, Wisconsin. By the 1940's it was also gaining popularity in Minneapolis and in the Seattle area of Washington. In the fifties, adult education classes in it sprang up in a number of communities, but even the teachers floundered for lack of models and direction.

It was to assist a movement looking for help that the Norwegian-American Museum in 1967 announced a national exhibition of Rosemaling in America and brought the painter Sigmund Aarseth from Norway to judge the works and give classes. The response was overwhelming. New painters from Norway were brought to Decorah every year, and eventually the exceptional painters in the American group were also asked to teach. For about ten years the demand for classes exceeded the Museum's capacity to offer them. More and more teaching began in areas outside Decorah, and by 1975 a full-fledged national movement was underway.

The policy at the national rosemaling exhibitions, which have been annual event since 1967, is to allow the winners to accumulate points: three for a blue ribbon, two for a red, and one for a white. After eight points have been earned, the painter is designated as a Gold Medal Winner and is excluded from

Objects at the National Rosemaling Exhibition sponsored by Vesterheim at the Nordic Fest, Decorah, Iowa. It is an annual event held the last full weekend in July.

Lila Nelson, Registrar and Curator of Textiles at Vesterheim, demonstrates spinning on an early Norwegian spinning wheel in the Museum collection.

Bergljot Lunde of Rogaland, Norway, demonstrates the decorating of a dowry trunk in a rosemaling workshop at Vesterheim.

5

further competition although still invited to exhibit.

The 24 artists who have reached Gold Medal status in the mid 1980's make up a core group in the American rosemaling world. Because of the great numbers of people now practicing the art and the high degree of competition at the exhibitions, there is also a great body of exceptionally competent and creative rosemalers who are still outside the Gold Medal group. To allow different styles to come forth and to allow recognition for talent that may not be strictly in line with old tradition, judges are seldom used more than once and the jury of three always includes an established artist from outside the area of rosemaling.

Although the Norwegian-American Museum has existed for over 100 years and assumes a wide range of responsibilities for the preservation of America's heritage from Norway, rosemaling has maintained a central place in its program since 1967. Two or three teachers are generally brought from Norway every year for 10 or more one-week workshops. The workshops by American painters at the Museum often double that number. Examples of early rosemaling brought to this country by the immigrants continue to be collected, and the best pieces characteristic of new developments in American rosemaling are generally purchased from the Exhibition.

There is no national rosemaling organization, but over 1200 rosemalers are kept in touch with each other through the Vesterheim Rosemaling Newsletter edited by volunteers living in the Decorah area. The painters have in common their enthusiasm for an art originating in Norway. Beyond that, they have come to represent a wide range of decorative styles. Originally the inspiration came largely from the region of Telemark, where a C-shaped scroll of Rococo character dominates. When Nils Ellingsgard from Hallingdal was brought to America as a teacher and judge in 1969, the more symmetrical style of that region gained prominence. The Hallingdal style has ever since been strongly represented among the rosemalers in Minneapolis.

Berglot Lunde of Rogaland in the early seventies acquired adherents for the precise and delicate forms of painting in that area. Among the followers of Lunde developed the first distinctively American style in rosemaling, commonly referred to as American Rogaland. A leading figure in this development is Vi Thode of Stoughton, and the style has continued to have a center in the Stoughton and Madison areas of Wisconsin. As a counterpart to it, a group of painters in western Minnesota led by Karen Jenson of Milan created a second American style with roots in the painting of Telemark. It is characterized by exceptional spontaneity and lyrical vigor with much wet-on-wet painting and with whiplash movements of the brush.

After the scholarly work of Nils Ellingsgard on all the major rosemaling styles of Norway was published in 1981, American painters have expanded their repertoires to cover the whole range of Norwegian decorative painting. Although most rosemaling is characterized by shaded scroll work, the breadth of form and expression encompassed by it is great. Floral motifs are the major subjects, but figures, birds, and animals also have an established place. They have come increasingly to the fore in recent American painting. This book is the first to cover the full range of rosemaling as it was developed in America.

His Majesty King Olav V of Norway greets members of the Vesterheim Board, on which he serves as Honorary Chairman. Behind him stands Marion Nelson, Director of the Museum.

American actress Celeste Holm admires a piece of rosemaling on a visit to Vesterheim.

Table of Contents

Vesterheim-Norwegian American Museum:
Membership Information
Pamela Publications:
"A Treasury of Norwegian Rosemaling"
Pattern Packet Information

This Book is Dedicated to:
The Norwegian Heritage and those who maintain its roots through
their artwork and interest in their culture.

A special thanks to:

Gary Albrecht — for his support and enthusiasm in conceptualizing and pulling together this project.

Dr. Marion Nelson — for his help and expertise not only with this book, but with Vesterheim, the Norwegian American Museum and what it represents.

Ethel Kvalheim — A most gracious and talented lady whose modest attitude and help made this a very rewarding project to work on.

Betty Dowe — For her hospitality, kind spirit, and assistance with promotion.

Honorary Mention for their Contributions: National Society of Tole and Decorative Painters, Dean Madden, Agnes Rykken, Norman Diamond, Diane Colavita

---

Published by Pamela Publications, a division of Pamela, Inc. ©1986

Pamela, Inc.
"exclusive Agent to the Folk Artist"
1117 Marquette Ave., Suite 1601
Minneapolis, MN. 55403
(612) 339-8139

Printed by:
Bolger Publications
3301 Como Avenue Southeast
Minneapolis, MN 55414

Cover Art:
Ethel Kvalheim

Technical Drawings:
Jill Fitzhenry

Technical Advisor:
Janet Rensberger

Photography:
Matthew Schmitt

Gary Albrecht

Gary Albrecht, artist, author and teacher, lives in Madison, Wisconsin. He and his wife, Renay, began a hobby of rosemaling in 1973 in order to decorate her father's Norwegian home near Iola, Wisconsin, the heartland of Scandinavian America. Inspired by his introduction to this art form, Gary continued to study the history and many varied styles of this unique folk art. He has, however, singled out the Rogaland style as his favorite because of its beautiful color blending and detail. He has studied with numerous prominent Norwegian and American artists. The texts he has authored include "A Treasure Chest of Rosemaling", "Traditional American Rogaland Rosemaling", "Rosemaling—Reflections on the Art", and "A Rosemaling Sampler—Volume I".

Numerous honors have been awarded to Gary for his works. He has received the coveted First Place Award at the National Rosemaling Exhibition, sponsored by Vesterheim in Decorah, Iowa. In this competition, he repeatedly won top honors among the more than 200 annual entries. His works are displayed in England, Switzerland, Hungary, Brazil, Argentina, Canada and Norway.

Teaching internationally is a very rewarding experience for Gary. It affords him the opportunity of extending rosemaling's ancestry and rebirth here in America. He takes pride in being a part of the development of a style of painting that uses the tenets of old rosemaling to create traditional "American" rosemaling.

As an artist, he encourages others to develop their own unique approach to the art form by entering the many rosemaling exhibitions and studying with as many painters as possible. He teaches regularly for chapters of the National Society of Tole and Decorative Painters as well as extension studies for the universities of Wisconsin, Minnesota and South Dakota. He is a member of the Wisconsin Rosemaler's Association, Norse Rosemaler's Association, Illinois Norsk Rosemaler's Association, Blair Area Rosemalers, Dairyland Decorative Painters and Sons of Norway. He has served as a judge for these associations' competitions.

Gary feels that in order to keep rosemaling alive today, it must be brought to the people who decorate in the market place. Gary and Renay operate a supply shop in Madison, keeping their students supplied with current market trends and supplies. They can be found together working at conventions for NSTDP and rosemaling exhibitions. He is proud to have participated in "Pamela Publications" Folk Art Designs, Volume I and Folk Art Borders Volume II. His travels have made him realize what an important job sharing the love of rosemaling really is. It is the encouragement from his students, who become friends, that provides the drive to create new life in today's rosemaling.

Awarded Gold Medal 1979

©G. Albrecht—1986

9

Eldrid Skjold Arntzen

A resident of Windsor, Connecticut, married to Arnt Norman Arntzen, mother of three and grandmother. I was born and reared in a Norwegian community in the Bay Ridge section of Brooklyn, New York. My parents were immigrants from the west coast of Norway, so I was always exposed to the Norwegian language, (learned to read and write it), and my Norwegian cultural heritage. Most of the rosemaling I saw was the commercially mass-produced work sent from Norway after World War II. When I was ten years old a teacher suggested that I be encouraged to take some sort of art lessons. I studied landscape and seascape painting with the Norwegian artist, Thorn Norheim, in Brooklyn. Music was also very important to me. During my teens I studied the violin as well as painting. Early in the 1960's I copied a rosemaling design from a card printed by Vesterheim. Sometime later I was invited to participate in a local arts and crafts show. I struggled to design and prepare a variety of rosemaled articles for that event. I was self taught until approximately 1971 when I began studying with Audrey Shine and Diana Boehnert in Connecticut. They introduced me to the New England Rosemalers' Society. After seeing their Rosemaling exhibit I was inspired to try harder. I became a member of the society in 1977. I have been actively painting and studying ever since. My husband and I have always promoted our cultural heritage. At his urging I decided to concentrate most of my artistic endeavors on Norwegian Rosemaling. In 1967 we obtained slides from the Norwegian-American Museum in Decorah, Iowa, and organized a fund-raiser at our Sons of Norway lodge to benefit the museum. These slides stimulated our interest in the museum. In 1979 we made our first trip to Decorah to experience the Nordic Fest. The big attraction for me was the Annual Rosemalers' Banquet and the National Rosemaling Exhibit. At the banquet slides from "The Akadamiet i Rauland" were shown. The exhibit was awe-inspiring, and the rosemaling bug really bit. I travelled to Telemark, Norway, in 1980 to study the Old Telemark style of rosemaling with Olav Fossli at the "Akadamiet". At the National Exhibit the following year I received a certificate of merit on a large bowl painted in this style. Since then I have been awarded three white and one red ribbon. Since 1981 I have travelled to Vesterheim at least once a year to study with visiting Norwegian rosemaling teachers. I have acted as interpreter (an interesting and learning experience.) I enjoy the challenge of learning different styles of rosemaling. The New England Rosemalers' Society has brought several teachers from the mid-west to teach and I have always taken advantage of the experience also.*

I joined the New England Rosemalers' Society in 1977 and have served as Vice-President and President for the society. I attained my professional status in the NERS in 1979. I have been teaching in my home and have conducted seminars in New England as well as in New York and Pennsylvania. I assisted in the organization of the Mid-Atlantic Rosemaling Society in Brooklyn, New York, several years ago and teach seminars there twice a year. I lecture and demonstrate Rosemaling for a variety of organizations. In 1985 I was invited by Lindblad Travel, Inc. to lecture, demonstrate and teach aboard the cruise ship, M/S Funchal, on its twelve-day North Cape cruise. It was a challenge with several different nationalities represented in the class. I teach at the Fletcher Farm School for the Arts and Crafts in Ludlow, Vermont, during the summer. I teach several different styles including Telemark, Hallingdal, Rogaland and Valdres, but I prefer the Telemark style.

Yankee Magazine featured an article about me early in 1982. In response to this article I have received letters from all parts of the United States as well as from England and Chile. I have had exhibits at libraries in this area and newspaper articles in Connecticut, New York, Pennsylvania, as well as "Haugesunds Avis" in Norway.

I played the violin in an amateur/professional orchestra for 10 years. I have always been a member of the church choir, and recently became the assistant choir director. I continue to work part-time as a Licensed Practical Nurse. I take classes whenever I can and work at the art full-time. I have done some restoration work also. Since 1982 I have been registered as a small business called "Nordic Designs".

Rosemaling is and continues to be a learning experience for me. It is an art form that allows me freedom of expression and creativity. I have learned to love rosemaling and I enjoy sharing it. We Arntzens are ardent enthusiasts about the United States, but we also believe in preserving our cultural heritage. One of the finest things that Norway has to share with the rest of the world is its art. I feel Americans should take what is good from their forefather's cultural heritage and share it, and that is what I am trying to do.

*Norwegian Teachers - Nils Ellingsgaard, Sigmung Aarseth, Olav Fossli, Sigrid Midjas, Tanja Westhagen, Hans Wold
American Gold Medal Teachers - Gary Albrecht, Karen Jenson, Dorothy Peterson, Ruth Wolfgram

Eldrid '86

Eldrid '86

Eldrid '86

Violet Christophersen

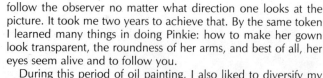

I was born in Marinette, Wisconsin, March 3, 1900. At the age of 3, I contracted a severe case of scarlet fever which left me extremely hard of hearing. My teachers were unable to get through to me. My mother taught me the alphabet and the pronunciation of words, and my father taught me numbers and the basics of arithmetic.

As a result of this handicap, I had no playmates because I could not reciprocate. My parents encouraged me to fill idle hours with drawing and simple watercolor painting.

In those early pre-teen years, I recall painting flowers on postcards which met with so much favor I sold them for 10¢ a dozen. This was a tremendous boost to an inarticulate emotional complex I lived with. Two years ago one of those very cards yellowed with age was presented to me by a resident at our Luther Home.

In my "teen" years I became involved in designing needlework patterns for embroidery work on pillowcases, dresser scarves, etc. Little did I dream this experience would prove invaluable to me many years later when I designed many stencil designs for textile painting on these very same projects. I was "drafted" to teach the art at our local Vocational and Adult School.

In 1936, I decided to take up lip reading for adults. We were often given 10 minute recess periods to rest our eyes. Invariably this would find me wandering the hall to watch an oil painting class. This was my first encounter with artist's oils and intrigued me to no end.

Due to my impaired hearing, I am a self taught person. I felt I could learn much by reproducing famous masterpieces such as Blue Boy or Pinkie. In the original, Blue Boy's eyes seem to follow the observer no matter what direction one looks at the picture. It took me two years to achieve that. By the same token I learned many things in doing Pinkie: how to make her gown look transparent, the roundness of her arms, and best of all, her eyes seem alive and to follow you.

During this period of oil painting, I also liked to diversify my spare time into Early American Gold Leaf work. It is a challenge which interests me to this day.

Along about the latter part of the 1950's there appeared a growing demand for a new art called "Rosemaling". Instructors were at a premium. I knew nothing about it. I was astonished to learn that it was a native art of Norway practiced by the Norwegians in the 17th and 19th century. How very interesting! My husband had many relatives in Oslo. An extensive correspondence soon followed with many helpful materials to come direct from Norway. Thus began a whole new career in Rosemaling.

In 1968, I was one of the first three top Rosemalers in the U.S.A. to win a gold medal at the Norwegian American Museum in Decorah, Iowa.

In 1970, I was a participant in the first of its kind "Rosemaling Tour" in Norway sponsored by the Museum.

In 1975, three of my works traveled in the land of Norway's own first traveling exhibition of U.S.A. Gold Medal winners.

In 1979, it was my privilege to prepare a Christmas card design by invitation from the Norwegian American Museum.

In 1985, at the annual Nordic Fest in Decorah, Iowa, I was presented with a second Gold Medal by the Museum.

Of all the arts it has been my opportunity to enjoy, Rosemaling has been the most rewarding. It has enriched my whole life beyond anything I ever dreamed of. For this I am deeply grateful to the Norwegian American Museum.

Awarded Gold Medal 1969

Violet Christophersen

Violet Christophersen

Betty Dowe

Although I was born in Davenport, Iowa, (June 21, 1936) to Jack and Olivia Keenan, I spent my youth in Johnsburg and Elgin, Illinois. In 1950 my parents moved to Pompano Beach, Florida, where my brother, Tom, and I spent our teen years. Following graduation from high school, I attended American School of Beauty Culture in Chicago, Illinois, and worked as a beautician until my retirement in 1963.

In 1958 I married Don, my high school sweetheart. We have four children: Debra, Marsha, Don Jr. and Greg, and a son-in-law, Chris.

Since my father was an artist, I have always been around oil painting. Living in Decorah leads a person to try various Norwegian arts and crafts. My interest and enthusiasm in rosemaling began when an adult education class in stained glass was cancelled and I enrolled in a beginning Rogaland class taught by Ruth Green. I found it challenging and a very exciting experience. A year later I took my first class at Vesterheim from Gary Albrecht. At Vesterheim I have studied with many Norwegian and American artists. I enjoy rosemaling in most styles, but Rogaland is my favorite. Although most of my work is done in oils, I have enjoyed painting with acrylics this last year.

Since 1980 I have been teaching rosemaling in Rogaland style. I was co-editor of the Vesterheim Rosemaling Letter from 1980 until the fall of 1985, when I became editor.

My family is very supportive of my artwork — my husband even does my backgrounding.

This year I will celebrate my fiftieth birthday and I will need at least another 50 years to accomplish all my rosemaling goals. I have especially enjoyed the beautiful people I have met through this fine art, and I really feel blessed.

Other interests include golf, teaching CPR, long walks, bridge, Beta Sigma Phi, projects for youth, church activities and warm weather!

Publications: ''Vesterheim Rosemaling Letter'' and ''Rosemaling Patterns for Christmas Tree Ornaments'' by Vesterheim

side

Betty Dowe '86

Porringer Design

top

back

Betty Dowe
"1986"

Carol Dziak

I was born and raised in Wisconsin, living in the Milwaukee area for over 40 years. I have always been interested in art and have worked in almost every medium. As a child, I spent most of my spare time designing clothes for my paper dolls and design still remains my first love.

After marriage in 1957, I began oil painting as a hobby, portraits being my favorite subject. Eventually, I branched out to sculpting and assorted other arts and crafts.

I began rosemaling in 1969 after a trip to Little Norway, Wisconsin. We were putting in a new kitchen and I thought rosemaling would be nice on the cabinets. One class led to another and the forming of the rosemaling association in Milwaukee and classes soon consumed all of my spare time.

I taught rosemaling for a time at Milwaukee Area Technical College, but soon tired of this. I found the students there, for the most part, were not serious about learning, but were looking for a night out, and next semester would be taking a sewing or cooking class. Those who are seriously committed to learning will take a week-long workshop and this is the type of class I prefer to teach.

I became a gold medal winning rosemaler in 1980. Shortly after that, my life changed dramatically. We moved to Michigan's Upper Penninsula where we spent two years refurbishing a 118-year-old historic hotel that has been closed for two years. The hotel was an overwhelming success, but harsh weather and 18 hour days were more than we cared to handle in our "old age".

We moved to Virginia in the fall of 1985. Our children had all left the nest and this was our chance to fulfill a dream of many years. We now own a small motel and a home in the Blue Ridge Mountains. The slower pace and warmer weather now afford us the time to do as we please.

I am now pursuing my interest in other art forms again and rosemale only on occasion.

I never did rosemale those kitchen cabinets, the reason being that I have never painted anything I was completely happy with.

Awarded Gold Medal 1980

Carol Dziak
86

21

C. DZIAK · 86

Diane Edwards

In 1970 my cousin and I climbed aboard a DC-8 and made the first voyage home to Norway by any of our family in over 60 years. It was a scary experience to get off a plane in a land so completely strange to our native plains of North Dakota—two young, naive and rather dumb prairie chickens in the middle of Oslo without a word of Norwegian beyond ''thank you'' and ''ja''! When we first stepped out on the tarmac we both had to fight the tears back of overwhelming emotion, and yes, already homesickness! It was somewhere in those few first days in Norway that I devoted some part of myself to everything that homeland stood for; somehow out of that experience came my total absorption in rosemaling. Even now I can close my eyes and smell the musty wood and feel the aura of personality that emanates from museums full of rosemaled history. I have been back to Norway several times and it still thrills me each time I enter an old building to see the glow of the warm rosemaling colors lighting up the dark interiors of the houses.

I was born on Norwegian Independence Day in North Dakota, in a Norwegian community where lutefisk and lefse were common foods and the May 17th celebrations were as important as Christmas and Easter. I was eight years old when I realized that the parties at church were not just for my birthday!!

In 1966 I graduated with a major in art and a minor in business. I was lucky enough to get a teaching job and haven't stopped since. I taught in high school for nine years covering K-12 as an art teacher and consultant. For four years I also taught some classes in music. I have always loved to play piano and organ and sing; everyone in our community sang, even on the radio! I have played for church for many years and directed a girls' chorus.

In 1972 I married Dale Edwards, who is a County Extension Agent, now in Grand Forks County. We have two children, Liesl, 12, and Brian, 10.

In 1976 we moved to Grand Forks from Newfolden, Minnesota, where we had both been teaching, and due to the fact that I couldn't find an interesting job, I opened my tiny shop (400 square feet at that time) and started teaching painting classes. I am now in my third location which is four times larger than my first place. This shopkeeping, however, has never been a prime interest of mine and I usually hire some helpful person to do all the hard work so I can just paint! In the last four years I have done a lot of interior decorating; I paint right on the walls with whatever they want done. I have painted anything from murals to roses and ribbons. It's great fun, but also hard work! I have painted two McDonald's restaurants, a motel, a ski lodge, parts of our church and many bedrooms and hallways.

Usually I teach about five classes a week and one or two out-of-town workshops a month. I love to teach and my biggest thrill is to teach at the NSTDP Conventions starting with San Francisco in 1982. My biggest frustration is that I only get to have them in class for a few hours. Although I have taken classes in many styles of rosemaling, Telemark is my favorite style. I enjoy the freedom and creativity of it. My first teacher in that style was my friend, Jackie Klokseth, who died in 1980.

My goals for the years ahead are to do more writing, designing and to continue my research and study of rosemaling. I love going to Decorah to take classes and feel as though it's my hometown. I urge anyone who is interested in rosemaling to go through the museum; it's almost like a quick trip to Norway. Those who are interested in rosemaling should realize how important history is to the art form and how technique is just an incidental part. Although it is important to paint well, it is necessary to know WHY you do each stroke. I also feel that we mustn't let all those Old Masters down—keep studying!

Diane Edwards
1986

Diane
Edwards
1986

Rhoda Fritsch

For Rhoda Fritsch of Aurora, Illinois, rosemaling is a family affair. "My husband, Al, does the sanding and staining," she says. "My daughters, Susan and Carol, seal and varnish. I do the designs and the strokework."

Rhoda Fritsch's family business grew out of a ten-year-old hobby of Norwegian Rosemaling. She works full time at her art. Her husband is also an air traffic controller; her daughters attend school at Aurora University and Aurora Christian High School.

Formerly an operating room nurse who grew up on a small farm in northern Minnesota, Rhoda took a tole painting class in a craft store when her girls were small. There she was able to study with several national master teachers, including Joan Johnson and JoSonja Jansen.

Soon she enrolled in her first rosemaling class. "I loved rosemaling," she recalls. "I enjoyed the colors and the graceful lines." But one class didn't satisfy Rhoda. She has since studied with many American rosemaling teachers, including Elma and Thelma Olsen, Dorothy Peterson, Vi Thode, Trudy Wasson, and Ruth Wolfgram. She also learned from Norwegians, Gunnar Bo and Berglot Lunde.

She joined The National Society of Tole and Decorative Painters. She became a charter member of both The Illinois Prairie Painters and The Illinois Norsk Rosemalers. She is an associate member of the Norwegian-American Museum in Decorah, Iowa.

Rhoda has entered her work in competitions at Geneva, Illinois, and Milwaukee, Wisconsin. She has also entered the national competition in Decorah, Iowa. "I won several ribbons in Geneva," she says, "Best of Show, People's Choice, and many other placements in the professional division."

Her work met with such enthusiasm that she began to teach classes and give demonstrations. Five years ago her business developed.

Rhoda takes custom orders and paints traditional wooden items for the Svenska Stuga Butik, in Libertyville, Illinois, and Lake Geneva, Wisconsin. She also sells art at The Country Folk Art Festivals in St. Charles, Illinois, and Kansas City, Kansas.

Her favorite style of rosemaling is Rogaland, either symmetrical or asymetrical, painted in the technique used in Norway today. Besides rosemaling, she also enjoys calligraphy and other fine old folk art forms.

RHODA FRITSCH - 1986

Ruth M. Green

I have been interested in art since I was a child and this interest led me to pursue an art major while attending college. I was introduced to rosemaling though an adult education class; in 1977, however, after moving to Decorah, Iowa, I became acquainted with the Rogaland style taught by Vi Thode in a class at the Norwegian-American Museum. It must have been "love at first sight," because I decided this was how I wanted to paint. I started practicing this style, particularly enjoying the rich color blending and symmetrical designs.

What began as a hobby eventually has become a full-time business. In addition to painting commissions and teaching rosemaling, my husband also became involved through his hobby of woodworking. He began by making some items for me to paint, and this led to making woodenware for others as well. After deciding that the wood and painted items were beginning to take over our home, we moved to a building that now houses woodenware and my studio. We have been operating our shop since May, 1985.

After studying with Gary Albrecht, I became acquainted with NSTDP and that association has opened up more of the world that includes folk art and decorative painting. I have been privileged to teach at the NSTDP national conventions since 1984 and have also taught at the Heart of Ohio Tole conventions in Columbus since 1983. In addition to teaching locally, including at the Norwegian-American Museum, I conduct seminars in other areas as well.

I publish pattern sets of Rogaland designs and have had four articles published in the "Decorative Arts Digest." I was co-editor of the Vesterheim Rosemaling Newsletter for five years. The letter is published under the auspices of the Norwegian-American Museum and goes to rosemalers throughout the United States and several foreign countries.

The study of rosemaling has helped me gain a better appreciation of my Norwegian heritage. With the Museum close at hand, it provides much inspiration, both in the collection it houses and the opportunities it provides in bringing Norwegian and American rosemaling teachers to conduct classes. The rosemaling that I have been fortunate enough to view, because of the Museum, has given me many ideas for designs that I can then adapt to fit the way I paint. I find that rosemaling offers a creative outlet as well as a chance to find my "roots" in that all my ancestors came from Norway. What was taken for granted as a child, now has taken on new meaning as I learn more of the Norwegian people and their culture through the study of rosemaling.

My family has been most supportive of me as I have pursued this area of my life. My husband and three children have always offered their encouragement. In addition, I find much enjoyment in the friendships that have been made because of rosemaling. The students, both those with whom I have attended classes and those I have taught, share a common bond that brings much enrichment and joy to life. Because of these things, rosemaling will continue to be a way of life for me.

~ruthgreen~

~ ruth green ~

Welcome to our home

~ruthgreen~

Barbara Hawes

Grand Rapids, MI

*I*n every painter's background there is always the path of color and brush which leads from first awareness to the present. As a child I was interested in paint and paper and as a teenager, I made various crafts which I sold through a local department store. My first professional job as a decorator came with the John Widdicomb Furniture Company of Grand Rapids, Michigan where I painted flowers on bedroom furniture. Eventually, I also painted furniture for Carlton Surry and the Baker Furniture Company and then I became a designer and advertising artist for a large department store.

My initial appreciation for folk art came with an interest in Early American tinware which I "discovered" while living in Boston soon after my marriage. When I acquired a copy of *Early American Decoration* by Esther Stevens Brazer, I began painting tinware for myself and it didn't take long before I was hooked on folk art! About that time I met Peter Hunt in Cape Cod. He had seen my work and asked me to paint for his shop in Orleans, Michigan. Busy Years!

Eventually, my husband and I returned to Michigan where I began teaching classes. I joined local art societies and exhibited at juried art fairs. Since my husband has a strong artistic background and both my daughters were by this time involved in various creative art, I found it natural and easy to keep painting — especially with a supportive family. My interest in folk art just kept growing and then I discovered Rosemaling!

One of the big highlights of my painting career came about in 1969 when I was able to attend a week's seminar with Sigmund Aärseth in Decorah, Iowa. What a privilege! He helped me define my rosemaling abilities and that same year I entered the rosemaling competition at the Norwegian American Museum in Decorah and won my first ribbon. The next year, I was awarded two more ribbons and then in 1971 I became the sixth American to win the Gold Medal Award for Rosemaling. That was a happy time for me.

Since then, I have been a featured artist in *Rosemaling in America Today, 1973;* I've been a contributing artist to *Rosemaling Patterns* by the Norse Rosemaling Assn.; exhibited my work in Norway; been featured on several educational television programs; demonstrated numerous times at ethnic fairs and festivals in Michigan; taught rosemaling for many years and today I am still contributing new pieces of my work each year to the annual rosemaling event at Vesterheim in Decorah.

Rosemaling has been a continuing interest of mine as it has allowed me to utilize my imagination and creativity in wonderful ways. Even though these days I do some original quilting for my family and church, I still consider myself primarily a painter. And I still love it!

Awarded Gold Medal 1971

Barbara Hawes · 1986

19 Barbara Hawes '86

Karen Elizabeth Jenson

Education: 1985: Atelier Lack, Minneapolis, Minnesota
1973-1985: Studied annually under Norwegian instructors at Vesterheim
1972: Addie Pittelkow, National Gold Medalist, St. Paul, Minnesota

Planned and Conducted Study and Research Travel Tours:
1983-1985: Guided work study tours throughout Norway and Sweden visiting old farm homes, museums and artists studios.

Teaching:
1973-1986: Have conducted classes in Iowa, Wisconsin, North Dakota, South Dakota, Minnesota, California, Connecticut, Canada, and New York

Awards:
1981: Best of Show, National Rosemaling Exhibit, Decorah, Iowa
1979: Gold Medal, National Rosemaling Exhibit, Decorah, Iowa
1979: First and Second Place, National Rosemaling Exhibit, Decorah, Iowa
1978: First Place, National Rosemaling Exhibit, Decorah, Iowa
1977: Second Place, National Rosemaling Exhibit, Decorah, Iowa
1976: Third Place, National Rosemaling Exhibit, Decorah, Iowa

Commissions:
1986: Zion Lutheran Church, Litchfield, Minnesota
Two 20 foot murals, one of the nativity and the other the crucifixion and resurrection of Christ, bordered by 60 feet of rosemaling and lettering
1985: Combined work on a painting with nationally known wildlife artist, Les Kouba
1984: Clarkfield Lutheran Church dining hall, Clarkfield, Minnesota

1984: Green Lake Bible Camp, Spicer, Minnesota
Eleven contemporary panels, combining figures with traditional rosemaling
1980: Kviteseid Church, Milan, Minnesota
Four washroom murals
1978 and 1981: Main Street Storefronts, Hayfield, Minnesota
1979: Breen Pharmacy, Benson, Minnesota
Wall mural with rosemaling
1979: Scandia Office Center, Willmar, Minnesota
Two wall murals with rosemaling
1979: Communion Set, American Lutheran Church National Convention
1970's: Blue Cloud Abbey, Marvin, South Dakota
Several communion vessels
1975: First Federal Savings and Loan, Glenwood, Minnesota
Ceilings, wall panels, door and furniture
1974: First Federal Savings and Loan, Madison, Minnesota
Ceilings, wall panels, door and furniture
Several pieces in the private collection of Vesterheim Museum, Decorah, Iowa
Numerous other pieces in private homes and public buildings

Exhibits:
1986: State Capitol, St. Paul, Minnesota
Photo Exhibit, organized by University of Minnesota Art Museum
1985: University Art Museum, Minneapolis, Minnesota
In observance of 20 years support for folk art programs by the National Endowment for the Arts
1974-1985: Nordic Fest, Decorah, Iowa
1981-1982: Gallimaufry, St. Cloud, Minnesota
1980-1981: Floyd Johnson Gallery, Minneapolis, Minnesota
1978: Southwest Minnesota Arts and Humanities Council, Traveling Show
1976-1982: Blue Cloud Abbey, Marvin, South Dakota

Awarded Gold Medal 1979

37

Ethel Kvalheim

My parents were of Norwegian ancestry. My husband was born in Norway. I have two married sons and five grandchildren who live in Stoughton.

I started painting several years ago. A neighbor, Per Lysne, was doing rosemaling. He taught very few people, I was not one of them. I visited his shop several times but the only information I got was what I observed. It looked easy so I thought I'd try. It was not easy and proved to be very frustrating. There were no books or teachers available. How lucky we are today with our wealth of material. I did not know what rosemaling was supposed to look like and today I am still searching. That is the intriguing aspect of the art. I did notice eventually that Per used certain brush strokes to create his designs. Frustration seemed to foster determination. The brushes I had were camel hair and the paint was enamel plus a few tubes of oil paint to mix extra colors. Whenever I heard of someone having old original rosemaling I asked to see it. Sometimes friends or a neighbor would let me borrow the piece. I made a trip to Decorah to study at the museum for a day. Finally some folios came out of Norway. These proved to be exciting and valuable information.

My first instruction came when I attended Sigmund Aarseth's class at Decorah. More frustration having to unlearn many bad habits and trying to learn a new type of design and technique at the same time. Since then this has been true with each new teacher I have studied with. I have taken classes with many of the teachers from Norway and learned from all of them.

Few pieces meet my expectations. It is the trying that is the thrill. The one that stands out as the happiest is the decorating of the Home Savings building here at Stoughton. The one I worried about the most was the Christmas card I made for the museum a few years ago. It sold out before Christmas.

Each year I do a Christmas card for Nelson Industries here at Stoughton. For several years I have painted a trunk for our 17th of May celebration. I try to paint for three shows a year, Decorah, Milwaukee, and Stoughton. Most of my time is spent in the study of the art, painting only what I want to paint.

The rosemaling tour to Norway in 1970 was the highlight of my rosemaling career.

I am a gold medalist awarded by the museum at Decorah. I have had writeups in several magazines, Ideals, Wisconsin Trails, Better Homes and Gardens Craft, Vinland and the Norwegian Familien. I received the Winsor and Newton "Best of Show" award in 1982 and 1985 at Decorah. While I am the recipient of the St. Olav Medal I feel I share this recognition with all rosemalers who wish to preserve the Norwegian heritage and culture.

Why do I do rosemaling? Guess it's like mountain climbing because it's there. The mountain of woodenware gets larger and more interesting each year. Years ago it was difficult to find a plate to paint on.

It's the people I have met that has made rosemaling so interesting for me. They are my friends.

Awarded Gold Medal 1969

Ethel Kvalheim 1986

Ethel Kvalheim
1986

1986   Ethel Kvalheim

Irene Lamont

In trying to find a beginning point to this biography, I was reminded of the day I walked into the public library in Marinette, Wisconsin. My husband, Bob, and I had recently moved to Menominee, Michigan, and he was beginning his vocal music teaching career at their high school. I wondered what life would be like in a small town after having lived in Minneapolis with all its cultural opportunities. I had taken some design classes at the Minneapolis School of Art and Design. This ongoing interest in art had brought me to the library. There was a rosemaling exhibit and I had come to find out just exactly what rosemaling was! The exhibiting artist was none other than Violet Christopherson. I was so excited about it that I immediately signed up for one of her classes at the local vocational school. How fortunate I was to be able to study with a Medal of Honor winner from the very beginning. Imagine having to go to Marinette to find out there was a Norwegian art form alive and flourishing in the Midwest. That visit to the library exhibit began a long and continuing love affair with rosemaling.

After six years in Menominee, we moved to Kaukauna. Again I found myself in a new community with new doors to open. The coordinator of the local vocational school asked me if I would teach a rosemaling class. My husband encouraged me to do so, and before I could think about it, I said yes. Violet's suggestion to study the old folio pictures was very good advice. They were an unending source of inspiration. I soon realized, however, that I needed more training to keep my students' interest. Sigmund Aarseth was scheduled to teach a one-week workshop in Door County. I took advantage of the opportunity and he opened another door for me — no patterns and using a transparent technique. After one week of "putting on and taking off" oil paint on a panel, I had only one panel to show my husband. There he was in the driveway, waiting for me to unload ALL my week's efforts. What I learned that week was something that could not be explained without having experienced it. It was not the actual project that was important, but rather the information that would help me grow in a new direction. Each succeeding summer I made a trip to the Vesterheim Museum to study with the Norwegian painters: Nils Ellingsgard, Sigmund Aarseth, Knut Anderson, Hans Wold, Bergljot Lunde and Gunnar Bo. I also studied with Dorothy Pederson, Vi Thode and Karen Jenson.

Last summer was a special year for me. I went to Norway and stood on the land where my great grandparents lived in Hoven, Telemark. We also studied West Coast rosemaling. On my return, I taught a one-week workshop at the Museum. Later, at the Nordic Fest, I was to have yet another treat — received an additional four points at the National Rosemaling Show, which qualified me for the Medal of Honor.

I have also taken up bentwood box making and carving. I hope to combine this into one-of-a-kind collector items. There is a real satisfaction in having started with a piece of wood, sawing, gluing, carving and painting a piece. My father and brother are carpenters, and as far back as I can remember, I would follow my father around, picking up scraps of leftover lumber and painting on it. I used greeting cards for inspiration. Later I turned to canvas painting. An oil painting titled "Teddy" was selected by Aaron Bohrod for the University of Wisconsin Extension Art Award for outstanding work, and it was on exhibit throughout the U.S. in 1972. My favorite pastime is still Rosemaling, however. I have concentrated on a simplified style of Telemark painting, using a limited palette. My main concern is to arrive at a unified whole; everything else is secondary. The style of painting is not as significant as the overall design.

Awarded Gold Medal 1985

Irene Lamont '86

42

Irene Lamont '86

Jan Loomis

began painting in 1965 taking my first class at the Y.W.C.A. at a time when there was little interest in Folk Art. There were only two teachers in our area, one a former china painter and one a former furniture decorator.

One year later I was teaching at the Y and loving it. I also started teaching adult education classes and also held classes in my home. I am still teaching and now have a lovely loft studio over our garage.

I became interested in Rosemaling soon after I started painting and traveled to Decorah several times, where I took classes from Sigmund and Nils. They have been a great influence with their free flowing style.

In competition at the Norwegian American museum in Decorah, I have one blue and three white ribbons to my credit. I also won Best of Show at the Norsk Association in Wisconsin.

I have taken classes in Folk Art whenever possible and my interest led me to take private lessons from one of the leading old masters in furniture decorators and designers in Grand Rapids. He taught me Chinoeserie and I now do consignment pieces.

I also published two books of designs some years ago and would like to do another of my favorite designs some day.

I keep very busy painting for gift shops. I painted for over 10 years for one shop.

Most of the designs I do are free hand and my own, but I must look back and say thank you to all those I was fortunate to take classes from.

I have a wonderful husband, Bob, and two daughters, Susan, 29, and Tracie, 26. Susan is a school teacher and married. Tracie owns her own business, a Title Company in Massachusetts. We are very proud of both our girls and our son-in-law.

Gyda Paulson Thoen Mahlum

It's a blessing to be of Norwegian descent and to have a small part in the preservation of Norwegian heritage in America.

My ancestors emigrated to the beautiful farm country of Iowa County, Wisconsin, from Ringerike, Hadeland, Telemark and Valdres, and the Norwegian language and customs were kept alive in our home. My interest in rosemaling came about after seeing work by the late Per Lysne of Stoughton, Wisconsin. As one of the early rosemalers in America, I was mostly self-taught with the aid of the Rogaland prints from Norway by Knut Hovden. My interest in rosemaling pushed into the background other interests in crafts, such as oil painting, watercolors, ceramics, china painting and needlework.

My life as a farmer's wife was busy, but I still found time for church activities, gardening, and attending adult craft classes at the Beloit, Wisconsin, Vocational School. My rural school teaching background gave me the skills to teach art classes in my home.

I have rosemaled pieces for the gift shop at Little Norway near Blue Mounds, Wisconsin, and I have published several sheets of rosemaling patterns, a brief manual with comments, and Norwegian sayings with translations.

I was excited when I received word that the Norwegian-American Museum, Decorah, Iowa, would conduct a rosemaling exhibit in connection with its 90th Jubilee in July, 1967, and was elated to receive a white ribbon on my blue tile entry. Included among other awards which I have won since that time are a red ribbon in 1968 on a blue plate which was purchased by the Museum, and the Gold Medal Award in 1972 on a blue plate which was also purchased by the Museum and which is included in the folder "Rosemaling in America Today." In 1969, I won the blue ribbon at the Wisconsin Show in Stoughton.

I was selected to represent Wisconsin at the National REA Convention Craft Show in Dallas, Texas, in 1973 to exhibit and demonstrate rosemaling as a craft which is characteristic of Wisconsin.

I was fortunate to be on the craft tours to Norway in 1970 and 1973 sponsored by the Museum. As a member of the Valdres Samband, I toured the Valdres Valley in 1976 and saw the traveling show of "Rosemaling in America" at Fagerness which included three of my pieces.

My design was the winner for the Commemorative Tile for the First International Convention of Sons of Norway held in Madison in 1982.

In 1985, I was one of several women honored during Women's History Week in Rock County, Wisconsin, for those who have achieved goals or made a significant impact on their friends, family, community or world.

In addition, I have judged national and state rosemaling shows along with a team of judges, and have participated in craft exhibits in Minnesota, South Dakota and Wisconsin.

I have been fortunate to have been in the rosemaling classes at the Museum every year since 1967, studying under Sigmund Aarseth, Nils Ellingsgard, Knut Anderson, Ruth Norbo, Bergljot Lunde, Olaf Tvieten, Gunnar Bo, Olaf Fossli, Oskar Kjetsa, Karen Jenson, Sigrid Midjas, Tanja Westhagen, Hans Wold and Ida Björgli. I am a life member of the Norwegian-American Museum, and belong to both the Wisconsin State Rosemaling Association and the Norse Rosemalers' Association, Milwaukee Area.

After my husband's death in 1980, I moved from the Luther Valley Area of Rock County, Wisconsin, to the village of Orfordville, Wisconsin in 1982, and still spend much of my time in rosemaling.

It is always a thrilling time for me to return to Decorah for the Nordic Fest, to be in a class, to greet friends and to meet new rosemalers. These past years have been a most interesting and rewarding experience.

Awarded Gold Medal 1972

1986

Gyda Mahlum

48

Gyda Mahlum
1979

Sunhild Muldbakken

Although Rosemaling is a Norwegian folk art, you don't need to be Norwegian to enjoy this beautiful form of art.

I was born in a German community in Sachsisch-Regen, Rumania, 46 years ago. I am the second of eight children born to Gustaf and Charlotte Schwab. We had to leave Rumania in 1943 because of the Russian occupation; then lived in Austria as D.P.'s (displaced persons) until 1951, when the Schwab family immigrated to the United States. A Lutheran congregation in Lamesa, Texas, sponsored us and my father found work there as a carpenter. Meanwhile, my aunt and her family immigrated to Sioux Falls, South Dakota. In order to be closer to relatives, my family also decided to move to Sioux Falls in 1953.

I met Odd at an International Friendship club meeting in the summer of 1958 and got married in 1959. We have three children, Rolf, 25, Deborah, 24, and Greg, 21. Rolf and Deborah are employed in Sioux Falls and Greg is a pharmacy student in Tucson, Arizona. I feel very fortunate because my husband and sons are able to make a lot of the wooden items I decorate.

My interest in rosemaling started in 1968 when my husband, Odd, and I went to Valdres, Norway, to visit his parents. After seeing this beautiful folk art in museums and homes, I knew this was an art form that I would want to try, since I had always enjoyed drawing and painting.

I started to take lessons in rosemaling in 1970 and have continued my instructions on a regular basis since then. I have been fortunate to have had the opportunity to study with some of the finest rosemalers in this country and also with those who have come from Norway. Although I enjoy painting different styles, the Telemark style of rosemaling has become my favorite.

I received my first award, a blue ribbon, at the Nordland Fest in Sioux Falls, in 1975. This encouraged me to enter the competition in Decorah, Iowa, in 1976. To my delight, the red and blue Telemark platter won me a white ribbon, which started me off to my eventual goal of getting the gold medal in 1984.

Although I have been fortunate to have received quite a few ribbons on my rosemaling, both locally and nationally, there have been a few that were especially meaningful. One came in 1979 when the Norwegian-American Museum in Decorah purchased one of my platters for the Vesterheim collection. Probably the biggest thrill was receiving a blue ribbon in 1980 on a big bowl in national competition in Decorah. Being presented the Viking Grand Award for Excellence in Rosemaling by the Nordland Fest Association was also very special.

My rosemaling has received exposure in the media through television, radio, and newspaper interviews; also in publications in the March, 1979, issue of Women's Circle, and the Valdres Samband Budstikken, December, 1980.

I started to teach rosemaling in 1973 with an adult education class in Sioux Falls. Since then I have had many workshops and demonstrations throughout South Dakota. Some have been co-sponsored by the South Dakota Arts Council.

Rosemaling has given me a lot of pleasure and the opportunity to meet a lot of wonderful people, and also the satisfaction in sharing this beautiful art form with my students.

Awarded Gold Medal 1984

Sunhild M.
1986

Sunhild M. 1986

51

Sunhild M. 1986

Thelma and Elma Olsen

When Thelma and Elma Olsen, twins living in Elkhorn, Wisconsin, were teen-agers, they studied oil painting. From the time they were little girls in first grade, they have been interested in art work of all kinds and received blue ribbons at the State Fair for their free-hand paper cuttings. Unusually skilled with their hands, they have since found many other mediums of expression. They had fun making paper dolls with complete costumes for many little friends. They have worked in watercolor, silhouettes and plastics. Always, they were looking for new ideas. One day, they visited Per Lysne of Stoughton, Wisconsin, whose name had been linked with the art of rosemaling for many years. Here, they found, was a type of art distinctive to their own nationality. It was one that offered a chance for unlimited originality and expression. They set out to learn this ancient type of Scandinavian decoration. Through some friends, they got in touch with a family in Norway and from them they received many fine color plates of valuable museum pieces decorated with authentic Norwegian design. They used these designs for ideas only. In the area of Elkhorn, the Olsen Twins were the only ones doing rosemaling for many years. Publicity in local papers and the "Wisconsin Agriculturist" and a national magazine "Profitable Hobbies" brought more interest and a trip to Norway in 1967 gave them more inspiration. Then, lessons from 10 different Norwegian artists who came to the Norwegian-American Museum in Decorah, Iowa, spurred them on and also made them "unlearn" some of their self-taught methods. They were encouraged by friends to enter rosemaling competions. The twins have always enjoyed painting together and they both paint on the same piece. For this reason, they have always entered competitions together. They have exhibited in State and National shows and have received about 30 ribbons and awards. In 1980, they received the distinguished gold medal award from the Norwegian-American Museum in Decorah, Iowa.

In 1969, the twins started teaching at Gateway Technical Institute in Elkhorn and over the years have conducted workshops and seminars in Naperville, Galesburg, Waukegan, Rockford, Illinois, and at Sister Bay in Door County, Wisconsin. Also, it might be noted, that in 1969 they did the illustrations for the Pioneer Cookbook as a volunteer project for the Museum at Decorah.

In the summer of 1978, they took a trip to Norway, sponsored by the Norwegian-American Museum and were privileged to study Rosemaling for two weeks at the Rauland Academy in the Telemark area. They had the opportunity to study under the best Rosemaling artists in Norway and to visit and sketch in the old farm homes in Telemark, where the old, original rosepainting from the 18th and 19th centuries is being preserved. In Norway, the Government is preserving and protecting collections so that the country may save some of its individualistic work for posterity. In America, Vesterheim, (The Norwegian-American Museum) has been very instrumental in promoting the quality and appreciation of rosemaling over the years, through educational programs, exhibitions and study tours. Thelma and Elma feel very grateful to be able to take advantage of these programs and to share with others what they have learned and continue to learn about this lovely art.

Awarded Gold Medal 1980

Olsen Twins
1986

olsen Twins
1986

Olsen Twins
1986

Gayle Oram

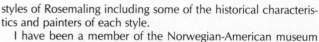

My first real exposure to art was while attending Oregon State University. As my education progressed it became increasingly important that I designate art to be my minor. At that time water color and architecture were the most interesting to me.

My first encounter with Rosemaling was while living in Petersburg, Alaska, a fishing community of predominantly Norwegian extraction. Arriving on the ferry I could see the "Sons of Norway" hall decorated with Rosemaling. Some of the businesses on Main Street, as well as some of the homes, were also decorated with the same theme.

My mother is also interested in art and was fortunate enough to attend a Pat Virch seminar in 1975. On one of her visits my mother showed me what she had learned and also left Pat's books with me. Although I was already teaching decorating painting, this was the beginning of my love for Rosemaling. I enjoy this style of decorative painting because it is a free-flowing, graceful form of painting that has many beautiful facets. It is relaxing and creative. I enjoy painting different styles, not just concentrating on one, because of the diversity they offer. As well as designing special wood pieces, I find it a challenge to take an object and create something special to decorate it.

I became increasingly interested in knowing and studying as much about the different styles of Rosemaling as I could. In 1983 my mother and I traveled to Norway to see it in its original forms. Vesla Harris was helpful in guiding my mother and I over the Telemark countryside to view various examples in their Norwegian settings. As a result I put together the book, "Rosemaling Gifts from Gayle," a book covering 13 districts and styles of Rosemaling including some of the historical characteristics and painters of each style.

I have been a member of the Norwegian-American museum in Decorah, Iowa, since 1980 and have participated in their annual Rosemaling exhibit. I also belong to the Northwest Rosemaling Association which is based in the Seattle-Tacoma area of Washington.

In 1975 I joined the National Society of Tole and Decorative Painters to keep in touch and learn more about the decorative painting field. The Society has played a big part in my life and in promoting tole painting and folk art styles of many countries (Norway, Sweden, Germany, Russia, England, Mexico, etc.) using a variety of methods, techniques and mediums. In 1980 I was awarded the title of "Master Decorative Artist" after passing the necessary requirements of the Society. I have served as a judge for the Certificiation program for four years and as a member of the Certification committee for two years.

"Christmas Gifts from Gayle" was the first decorative painting book that I published and it is now out of print. It included a sampling of Christmas customs and painted decorative items from a number of countries.

In 1985 I began a series of books entitled "Kitchen Gifts from Gayle" which includes different styles of Rosemaling, Hindelopen, and decorative painting on creative objects for the kitchen and entry to the back door. In addition to these publications, I have written articles published in the following magazines: The Decorative Painter, Decorative Arts Digest, Tole World, and Priscilla Hauser's Workbook.

I have taught through three community colleges at different places I have lived for a number of years. I also enjoy teaching Rosemaling and decorative painting nationally for NSTDP chapters and conventions as well as shops around the USA.

I have a great deal of gratitude for the encouragement the NSTDP and my fellow artists and Rosemalers have extended to me over the years.

Design for plate, box or clock face. Repeat border around or center top and bottom.

Repeat design to right side of center panel so angels are facing towards the center.

Repeat design to left side on outside panels so when the sides are turned in this area is visible.

Trudy Peach

I became interested in the art of rosemaling before you could find many classes offered in it. I suppose my interest in it had something to do with my Norwegian background. The first class I enrolled in was in 1969 at the Vo Tech in Milwaukee, Wisconsin, while my husband and I were living there. In that class we were taught to mix our artist oils with enamel paint for rosemaling. I did not continue to paint after this class, but I did keep my supplies. However, in 1974, after we had moved to Minneapolis, I saw rosemaling offered again through a Community Education program. This time my enthusiasm was spurred on enough to continue to paint and take additional classes. Since then I have taken several classes through the Norwegian-American Museum in Decorah, Iowa, studying with — Vi Hode, Gunnar Bo, Sigrid Midjas, Bergljot Lunde, and Addie Pittelkow. There is so much to learn in this beautiful art form that I anxiously await each time I can schedule in a class to be inspired all over again.

In 1984 I was fortunate enough to be able to go on the tour of Norway arranged by Sigmund Aarseth for the Norwegian-American Museum. It was a chance in my lifetime to see many wonderful pieces of old rosemaling and be able to photograph them so that I would have them to study over and over again.

I have instructed many rosemaling classes over the years and have rosemaled many different objects. I still get that exciting challenge with each new piece I paint. My family keeps me busy so I don't always find the time I'd like to spend painting. My children are ages 12, 11, and 1. My husband has been my biggest supporter and critic and has always given me that extra encouragement to keep on painting.

There are many good competitions held for rosemalers, but due to the limited amount of time I find to paint, I have only entered a few of them. One year I received the People's Choice Award when I entered the Minnesota Rosemaler's Association competition held at Augsburg College in Minneapolis. I have also received ribbons at Nordic Fest, the National Competition, held in Decorah, Iowa, and have also placed at the Terrace Mill Heritage Festival in Terrace, Minnesota. The Norwegian-American Museum has purchased two of the 16" plates I had entered in the 1980 and 1984 Nordic Fest competitions which are on display with the Museum's collection of rosemaled pieces. My family is especially pleased the Museum has these as each was painted with the intent of going into my husband's office. Now only seven years after his first request for a piece of rosemaling for his office wall, I am hoping again to paint a piece for him soon!

I am also honored that the Terrace Mill Foundation has purchased two pieces I entered in their rosemaling competitions. One piece is a 16" plate and the other is a serving tray. These are both displayed in their permanent collection as well.

Up until this date, I have spent most of my rosemaling years painting Rogaland style. However, I would like to expand and paint more in each of these beautiful styles. Sometimes I am surprised to think I'm doing artwork because I went to school for business — not art. However, color has always been a fascination for me and Rogaland style rosemaling does offer beautiful color.

Trudy Peach 1986

Trudy Peach ~ 1986

Trudy Peach ~ 1986

Dorothy Einer Peterson

Having been born and raised in southwestern Wisconsin, among loving family members of Norwegian heritage was a blessing. The introduction to rosemaling in the early years was through family heirlooms, but it was in 1967, in Ironwood, Mich. that my husband encouraged me to learn to paint. Leaving six children with their father to attend a five day workshop, opened the door to a new way of life. Theron thought that everything could be learned in one week, but the classes are still continuing because you never can stop attending classes if your life in the art is to continue.

In 1969, Nils Ellingsgard of Oslo, Norway, arrived at Vesterheim, the Norwegian American Museum in Decorah, Iowa, to teach his first class in America. This was my first experience with a Norwegian teacher and opened up a whole new world for me. Through the years I was part of 11 other classes with Ellingsgard, plus instructions from Sigmund Aarseth, Ballot Lunde, Gunnar Bo, Hans Wold, Knute Andersen, Ruth Nordbo, Oskar Kjestsa from Norway and Pat Virch and Vi Thode from America.

For many years my painting showed a great influence of Hallingdal style and the past few years I have broadened this art to include the lesser known styles, from Osterdalen, Valdres, Gudbrandsdal, Os and Hordland, Rogaland and Romsdal. Teaching in nine different states has provided both experience and good friends. Teaching at the Norwegian-American Museum has been both an honor and a privilege.

In 1975 I received the highest award in Rosemaling from the museum for exhibiting Rosemaling after seven years. The Gold Medal is a goal for all Rosemalers.

The interest in the Art made it possible to travel to Norway eight times, both for research and instruction. My husband and I also traveled through Europe and saw the folk art of other countries. Three of the trips to Norway were with tours sponsored by the museum. They definitely are an educational experience and should be recommended to anyone who really wants to see the beautiful country and meet the people and study the art and other crafts of the finest quality. The other trips were with friends, traveling by auto, visiting museums, and people living in Norway.

A great number of times, judging rosemaling shows has been offered to me. These exhibits of exceptional fine rosemaling were held in Stoughton, Chicago, Milwaukee, Western Wisconsin, South Dakota, Minneapolis, MN, as well as the National Show in Decorah. This gives a judge a good background and understanding of design, color balance, originality etc. of all painters.

Two years ago the Petersons purchased an old farm home in the area of Cashton-Westby Wisconsin area. It has been restored and has been decorated with rosemaling by Nils Ellingsgard. Our plans are to spend most of our time in this home when Theron retires after 35 years of teaching. This house is located close to my birthplace, near the valleys and ridges where my family settled after emigrating to America from Norway. It may be seen upon request to interested people, please write or phone ahead for a convenient time.

In the future I will continue to paint, teach and talk rosemaling. Meeting new friends, and promoting good rosemaling is very necessary, once you have been introduced to the history and art of rosemaling.

Awarded Gold Medal 1975

Dorothy E. Peterson 86

dEP. 86

Karen Jenson – 8' × 5' Dresser

Ethel Kvalheim – 17" × 27½" Trunk

Trudy Peach – 32½" × 20" Trunk

Eileen Riemer – 12 ⅞″ × 10″ Trunk

Carol Dziak – 16″ × 12″ Small Trunk

Elaine Schmidt – 24″ × 15″ Trunk

Betty Dowe – 24″ × 15″ Trunk

Gary Albrecht – 20" Plate

Sunhild Muldbakken – 21" Large Plate

Nancy Schneck – 34½" Plate

Gyda Mahlum – 15½" Plate

Thelma & Elma Olsen – 14" Plate

Ruth Green – 14" Plate

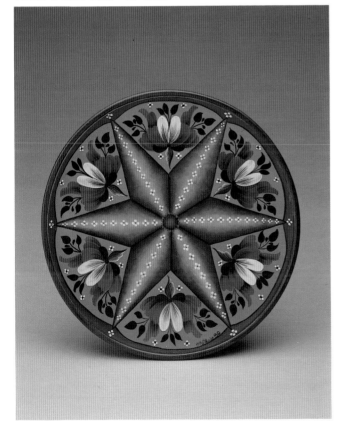

Vi Thode – 10" Small Plate

Dorothy Peterson – 11½" Clock

Eldrid Arntzen – 12½" Bowl

Barbara Hawes – 14½" Bowl

Claudine Schatz – 16" Bowl

Irene Lamont – 22½" Bowl

* Agnes Rykken – 11½″ Tina   Contributed by Vesterheim   Diane Edwards – 5½″ × 5″ Small Ale Pitcher

Norma Splitt – 10″ × 11½″ Large Ale Pitcher   Pat Virch – 16″ Tina

Gayle Oram – 17" × 22" Wall Pocket

Rhoda Fritsch – 15⅞" Bowl

Sheila Stilin – 12½″ Triangular Box

Violet Christophersen – 12″ Round Box

Margaret Miller Utzinger – 28″ × 29½″ Chair

Trudy Wasson – 14″ × 31″ Tilt Top Table

Jan Loomis – 27″ × 16″ Panel

Ethel Kvalheim

Irene Lamont

Carol Dziak

Violet Christophersen

Diane Edwards

Trudy Wasson

Elaine Schmidt

Thelma & Elma Olsen

Trudy Peach

Rhoda Fritsch

Gyda Mahlum

Barbara Hawes

Norma Splitt

Ruth Green

Karen Jenson

Dorothy Peterson

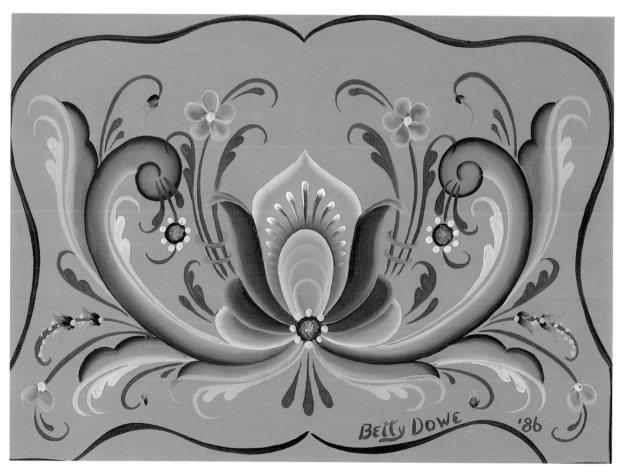

Betty Dowe

Vi Thode

Sunhild Muldbakken

Eileen Riemer

Claudine Schatz

Pat Virch

Gary Albrecht

Gayle Oram

Nancy Schneck

Margaret Miller Utzinger

Jan Loomis

Eldrid Arntzen

Sheila Stilin

Eileen Riemer

Originally from Austin, MN, our family moved to Milwaukee during the war years. I attended school in Milwaukee and West Allis, a suburb of Milwaukee. In high school, art was one of my majors. I love many types of arts and crafts, however, never able to find an area that I could really create my own style.

My husband Vic, and I met in school, were married and have raised four children and now have four grandchildren.

I started rosemaling at the YWCA in Waukesha, with Norma Hugdahl. It was in 1969, when she had recently come back from Sigmund Aarseth's first class in Decorah. She shared what she had learned from him plus her own style (no patterns). I spent many hours with a magnifying glass and any small picture I could study.

My next class was with Dixie Dillow. Dixie had many plates painted by Sigmund Aarseth. Each week we could use them to work with, but it was still a struggle.

In the early 70's Nils Ellingsgard came to Stoughton, Milwaukee, and finally Waukesha where I was able to attend his classes.

Sigmund also came to Milwaukee. I was able to purchase panels painted by both Sigmund and Nils. I finally had something to study. I still have them and still work with them.

Later I studied with Vi Thode, when she was teaching the Telemark style. A very good friend and I would drive to the Madison area once a week just to be in a half day class with Vi. She had so much to share.

I was able to purchase pieces of work from my favorite Rosemalers. I have them on display in my home where, when I look, I see good rhythmical work all the time.

I have also had a class each with Karen Jenson, John Gunderson and Oskar Kjetsa.

I did create my own style from working and learning with all these excellent Rosemalers and finally in 1977 received my Gold Medal Award from Vesterheim.

I still work to try to change and improve my style.

Recently I have begun to teach short workshops in my freehand style. I have met such friendly, thoughtful people doing this. I just hope I can give as much as I have received from those who were my teachers.

Attending Rosemaling Shows in Stoughton, Nordic Fest in Decorah, Geneva, IL, and Milwaukee is one of my favorite things to do. The quality and style of Rosemaling has come so far since 1969. There are so many, many good painters and so much good information and books now.

I am a charter member and past President (1982-1983) of the Norse Rosemalers Association in Milwaukee.

Doing designs for this book is a new experience for me. I hope everyone will enjoy them. Happy Painting.

Awarded Gold Medal 1977

Eileen Riemer
1986

Eileen Riemer
1986

Claudine Schatz

As far back as I can remember I have needed to make "pretty things" and this urge continues to dominate my life. Having learned needlework skills from my mother as soon as I was able to imitate her nimble fingers, I tried every handicraft that touched my life.

While our family of three were growing and becoming involved in all the activities of childrens' lives I was organizing, directing or teaching everything from Brownie Scout day camp arts and crafts, posters for Poppy Day, window displays for Red Cross fund drives, floats for celebrations or parades, to Christmas plays for Sunday School students—always in the role of "making something pretty".

Later I studied art at Upper Iowa University and thought I had found my niche, especially in the design classes. Then, I watched, fascinated, as Sigmund Aarseth of Volbū, Norway, demonstrated rosemaling at the Norwegian-American Museum, Decorah, Iowa, in 1967, and knew I had come home.

I was fortunate to be living near the Museum so each time a Norwegian teacher came over the horizon I was in class again. I have studied with 12 different Norwegian teachers, some of them many times. I also participated in three of the Museum sponsored study tours to Norway and constantly turn to those sketch books and albums of color prints of the old rosemaling that came out of those tours. There is always inspiration and learning to be found in the study of these materials.

Teaching followed as a natural result and for a number of years I loaded up the car and hit the road in Northeast Iowa and Southeast Minnesota. There were few arts and crafts shops at that time and the adult education programs in the various communities were the main resource centers for passing on this exquisite art form. Before long I began to cross more state lines and for a time crossed the country to teach at seminars and workshops.

In 1978 I met JoSonja Jansen and became another of her devoted students and my study of folk art now extends beyond the boundaries of the Museum and Norway. In 1980, after my husband's retirement, we moved to Northwest Arkansas into Tole and Decorative Painting country so another dimension is being added to my painting. In fact, the area flourishes with every kind of artistic expression you can imagine and I wish I could learn it all.

While I enjoy all styles of painting my favorite is still the round brush stroke technique of Hallingdal rosemaling. I appreciate the symmetrical design approach, the vibrant use of color and the luxuriant scrolls and flower forms found in this style of rosemaling. Even more than painting, however, my greatest pleasure has become the study and research that goes into the designing process.

And the teaching—the exhilaration (and sometimes exhaustion) of teaching! You can't be so enthusiastic about something and not tell someone else. So out of the teaching came the books—the requests of students to "write it all down" so they would have it for reference. It has been most rewarding to hear from painters in remote areas who do not have access to classes or teachers but have received help from the books.

I was an editor of Vesterheim Rosemaling Letter for three years before moving from Iowa and have made scores of friends from the painting of at least 1,000 rosemaled name tags for the Rosemaling Reunion dinners, Museum tour groups, and some Sons of Norway lodges. I've lectured, demonstrated, exhibited, judged, and painted on commission since 1970.

At the present time I am teaching rosemaling and Folk Art at various shops in the area, preparing for another lecture and out-of-state seminar. I am active in two NSTDP chapters and participate in two area art clubs.

I have also come full circle as I prepare to embark again in a new study of pastel painting. As much as I shall enjoy it, however, it will never supplant my beloved Hallingdal rosemaling.

Publications: Hallingdal Rosemaling, Vol. I and II; Rosemaling Roses.

Claudine Schatz - 1986

Claudine Schatz - 1986

Nancy Schneck

Contrary to logical reasoning, one doesn't have to be of Norwegian ancestry in order to be a successful Norwegian rosemaler. My ancestry is German, but I found that after moving to Milan, Minnesota, a predominantly Norwegian community, I couldn't lick them, so I joined them and I've had a lot of fun joining them.

I grew up in the very small western Minnesota community of Odessa. The high school closed after I graduated, if that tells you anything. My parents and my only sister have always been very supportive of me and my rosemaling, that is, after they found out what it was. They had never heard of it before I introduced them to it in the late 70's. My school years didn't include any art classes—so I've had to start from scratch learning color, design, etc. In those years, however my interest leaned toward medicine and nursing; so who knows whether or not I would have taken advantage of the art classes even if they had been available. Following high school, I went into nurse's training, then business college and held various jobs in both fields while getting my husband through the University of Minnesota Veterinary College.

We were married in 1968, he graduated in 1970. We lived in Cloquet, MN, for a year and then moved to Milan to organize our own veterinary practice. With my business background, I was able to do all the office work required and with my nursing background, I was able to assist with surgeries and exams as necessary. We have two daughters, ages 15 and 12. They are both very active and successful academically, musically, athletically and are very busy in our church activities. It keeps me very busy keeping them and their schedules together. It was a good thing I started painting when our children were young because now they demand more of my time which I am very happy to give them. My girls and my husband are most supportive of my artistic endeavor, and this is so very important. They take over all my cooking, cleaning and laundry duties for me when I am off teaching or taking classes.

In 1976, my husband gave me a very special Christmas gift—a trunk rosemaled by a dear friend, Sally Thompson. It was very lovely! The more I looked at it, the more I thought that rosemaling was something I would like to learn to do. So, the next year, I had a friend go with me to buy the paints and brushes that I would need. I worked on my own for a couple of months along with the help of the Aarseth-Miller book, a gift from my husband. Finally, I took an evening community education class from Karen Jenson and later a week long seminar from her. That gave me a very good start on the basics. Since then, I've painted in classes with American Gold Medalist Addie Pittelkow, an excellent teacher and a lovely person, and Norwegian artists Gunnar Bo, Nils Ellingsgard and Sigmund Aarseth. I am most familiar with Sigmund's style, but all three gentlemen are most exceptional individuals and painters. Working with the Norwegian painters adds such a unique dimension to the art, that a rosemaler must not miss the opportunity to take advantage of the Norwegian artist's talents when they are available to us.

In my rosemaling career, I've entered lots of shows and contests, and that, I feel, also adds a dimension to one's painting, in that one gets constructive critiques and ideas from varied knowledgable people in the field. Shows in this area that I have entered and received awards from include the Norse Rosemaler's Show, Nordland Fest, Terrace Mill Heritage Fest, Minnesota Rosemaler's Show and the National Show at the Nordic Fest in Decorah, Iowa. By 1984, I had earned enough points to be awarded the coveted Gold Medal of Honor; that is the highlight of a rosemaler's career. But even more important than that are the many friends that I have made since my rosemaling career began. Sometimes I don't see some of them for months or even years at a time, so our times together at the Fest or classes are very special.

In the last couple of years, I have taught classes in various parts of the country and that, too, has added a dimension for me, being on the other end of the brush, so to speak. All in all, rosemaling has opened lots of doors for me and I have met so many fine people and done so many fun things. I look forward to more of both!

Awarded Gold Medal 1984

Nancy
Schneck
1986

Elaine L. Schmidt

Hales Corners, WI

Born and raised in the Milwaukee area and educated in both public and parochial schools, I started my rosemaling career about 20 years ago by attending classes to paint a few pieces for my home; but my love for rosemaling grew and grew.

I entered my first rosemaled piece for competition in Stoughton's Rosemaling Exhibit in 1970 and won a blue ribbon on an 18″ blue plate, how thrilled I was. Then it was on to Decorah, Iowa, for the National competition in 1970 where I received an honorable mention. Through the years I have received numerous awards at various shows and am in need of one more point for my Gold Medal.

Being a charter member of the Norse Rosemaler's Ass'n. in Milwaukee, which formed in 1971, I entered their first show at the Y.W.C.A. in Hales Corners and received three awards. My love for Rosemaling kept me in the Association where I served as President from 1975-1977 and Treasurer, along with my husband Mel, in 1983-1985. Serving on various committees in this organization as the years progressed, has been a great incentive for me.

My teaching career started in 1972 at the Y.W.C.A. in Hales Corners and at Milwaukee Area Technical College, Greendale Campus, in 1975. Through the years, the teaching of numerous workshops here and in other states has added to my enjoyment as well as demonstration of Rosemaling at The Heritage Festival in Racine, Historic Walker's Point in Milwaukee, Allen Bradley Company, Milwaukee Libraries, church and local organizations. The drawing of designs both for myself and my classes has always been a highlight in my career. Giving my husband ideas for woodenware, which he so patiently creates for me, has also added another dimension to my career. When each semester of classes unfold, I look forward with great enthusiasm knowing I can in some way impart some knowledge of this great art to my students, many of whom have studied with me for a number of years, and I might add, have entered the winners circle in their own right.

I have studied with various Norwegian artists to whom I feel greatly indebted for the knowledge obtained from them. Amongst them are Nils Ellingsgaard, Sigmund Aarseth, Ruth Nordbo, Knut Andersen, Alfhild Tangen, Elsa Sjovaag and Bergljot Lunde.

My styles of rosemaling have varied through the years. My first love was Hallingdal, as this was the first style of painting that I was introduced to and for which I feel I have mastered and consequently received numerous awards. It was then on to Telemark which I find myself painting when I feel a desire to create a more free style of painting. Rogaland has also been a great love of mine. The dimensional look and depth of colors has always intrigued me in this style of painting and I feel I am more comfortable with symmetrical painting, maybe I can say I am more of a symmetrical style painter. However, I love all the styles of rosemaling as long as they are done well!

Having been invited to decorate beams, walls, doors and furniture pieces in various homes has been among my rosemaling accomplishments; but the greatest thrill was the interior of a restaurant in Slinger, Wisconsin.

Also, a great honor has been the judging of various Rosemaling shows through the years. The studying and painting of Hallingdal, Telemark and Rogaland, all of which I feel I have mastered, has given me a good background for judging. To be able to join with other mastered artists while judging is also a great thrill for me.

Some of my other past and present enjoyments have been fishing, hunting, snowmobiling, lots of golfing and traveling. Flower gardening has also been a great love.

My goals for the future are to keep creating, painting and teaching this beautiful art; and to my husband Mel and son Todd, I give much love for their many hours of support.

Elaine L. Schmidt - 1986

Elaine L. Schmidt - 1986

Elaine L. Schmidt — 1986

Norma Splitt

I was born in Opheim, a small prairie town near the Canadian border in northeastern Montana. Since 1928 central Wisconsin has been my home, where a long time interest in painting led to my discovery of the traditional Norwegian art of Rosemaling in the early 1960's. Classes offered at the local vocational school provided an introduction to Rosemaling and prompted a visit to the Norwegian American Museum in Decorah, Iowa. Through efforts of the museum, I have been a student in the Rosemaling courses offered by Norwegian instructors annually since 1969. Instruction was provided in the Hallingdal style of Rosemaling by Nils Ellingsgard, a Norwegian rosemaler from Oslo under whose guidance I have studied during each of his visits to the United States. This background led to my teaching of beginning Hallingdal courses at the museum for several years. Other Norwegian instructors I've studied under include Bergljot Lunde, Rogaland style; Knut Andersen, Olaf Tvieten, Olav Fossli, Oskar Kjetsaa, Tanja Westhagen, Hans Wold, and Ida Bjorgli, all in the Telemark style. Despite exposure to various styles of the Telemark instructors, my interest in Rosemaling is influenced most heavily by the Hallingdal tradition.

My individual works entered in national competition through the Rosemaling Exhibits offered by the Norwegian American Museum each year during Nordic Fest have earned ribbons including an undisputed first place on a table now displayed in the Museum. Through this competition I've compiled seven of the eight points toward the honor of being a Gold Medalist. Articles which I've Rosemaled have been purchased or commissioned for individuals and businesses throughout the United States, Canada, Italy, South America and Australia. My original set of notepapers featuring four designs is now in its fourth printing and the second set of notepaper designs is currently being printed.

I have shared my knowledge of Rosemaling and in particular the Hallingdal style with painters in the United States and Canada. Within the past 15 years I've offered classes through individuals and organizations including the Sons of Norway Lodge in the mountains of Washington; Redlands, California; Seattle, Port Angeles, and Tacoma, Washington; Victoria, British Columbia; Thunder Bay, Ontario; Coon Rapids and Sioux City, Iowa; Grand Rapids, Minnesota; and throughout Wisconsin. Demonstrations, exhibits, and lectures have been provided to organizations of Rosemalers and through the Sons of Norway. My commitment to the Norwegian American Museum has included volunteer work in fund-raising and special projects to enrich its cultural offerings. I currently am serving in my sixth year as a trustee on the Board of the Norwegian American Museum.

Norma
1986

Norma

Norma
1986

103

Sheila Stilin

Rosemaling was introduced to me in 1972 when I attended an arts and crafts show in a small community in northern Wisconsin. Dorothy Peterson was demonstrating the art, and as I looked at each piece of her work the more excited I became. Needless to say, I started taking classes from Dorothy as soon as they were available. I still take classes from Dorothy whenever I can.

I only took classes for about a year when our family moved from the small town of Mellen, Wisconsin, to Jackson, Mississippi—my husband and I and our three children and the great opportunity to learn about living in the deep South. We were there long enough to settle into a friendly neighborhood, when the call came from the John Deere Co. to move to Dubuque, Iowa. While living there we took a trip to Decorah naturally visiting the Norwegian-American Museum. The bug bit again. I was itching to get at the brushes when another move was on the horizon. This time it was to Rhinelander, Wisconsin. It was only 1974.

Luckily for me, an active Rosemaling group was already established in this neat little community. It has been through this group that I have made dear and lasting friends. A move couldn't have been more fortunate for me. Through a very supportive community college many of the great American Rosemalers came to share their talents with us. I took every class that was made available, and was saddened when the funding could no longer be provided. However I was determined to continue my education in the art of Rosemaling and now take classes at the Norwegian-American Museum when I can.

During this time our children are growing, we have stayed in one place, I went back to my nursing profession on a part time basis, and the painting table is always ready for me to sit down and move those brushes around.

As I look back on this, it's amazing that painting has become such a part of my life. Art in any form was low on my agenda of things to do. It has been a pleasant surprise.

The experience with Rosemaling has been something special in many ways. I would have never in my wildest dreams entered my work in any competitive exhibitions had it not been for painting friends prodding me. Attending those exhibitions opened a whole new world. Most specifically my spectrum of dear friends has broadened tremendously. Not only in the field of Rosemaling, but in many areas of decorative painting. What fun loving, kind and sharing people. Winning a few ribbons was an extra bonus, and it helps one to strive to do better. My personality seems to need that push, or I have this wonderful attribute called procrastination.

So, I continue my love affair with Rosemaling and its many facets. It has enriched my life and that of my family. By the way, I have no Norwegian heritage, however, my mother reminded me the other day that my maternal grandmother was Swedish. That may be dangerous to admit to my Norwegian friends, but it may bring a grin.

1986
Sheila Stilin

1986

Sheila Stilin

Vi Thode

I have been studying rosemaling for about 25 years and enjoying every minute of it. I began teaching about 2 years after I first started. I soon went to Decorah, Ia., to study with Sigmund Aarseth of Norway. Sigmund taught Telemark style. I studied three years with Sigmund at least one or two weeks each year. Nils Ellingsgard of Norway taught Hallingdal. I studied with him each summer for four years. Sometimes, I studied two weeks at a time.

For 14 years, I taught some Telemark but mostly Hallingdal in the vocational classes. During this time, I taught in northern Wisconsin in the summer. Also, each summer, I attended classes in Decorah, IA, either with Nils or Sigmund or any teacher coming from Norway.

In 1970, I traveled to Norway for a three-week tour of the museums and historical places—a trip I shall never forget. Also, the same year, I received the Gold Medal from Decorah. I think 1970 was the high point of my life. In 1973, I went to Norway again on another tour.

I was also chairwoman of the State Rosemaling Exhibit held in Stoughton, WI, each year around May 17 for 10 years. Again, three years later, I was the first president of a newly organized Rosemaling Association for the first year.

I am a life member of the Norwegian-American Museum at Decorah, IA.

For many years, my husband made wooden plates for rosemaling as I continue to do today. We sold this plate all over the United States and Canada, Norway, Germany and Italy.

My first publication was a folio of color plates and note cards. Another teacher, Bergljot Lunde, from Norway came to the museum in Decorah to teach the Rogaland style. I went to class and became so enthusiastic about this style, I came home and studied the design more, then began drawing new designs and teaching. I soon learned this could become something everyone could learn to paint. I had specific methods for mixing the paints, which we had never done until this time.

In 1977, I published a book called "Rosemaling Instructions" mostly concerning the Rogaland style of painting. This was a good-sized book and my last as far as I was concerned. But, in 1978 a beginners book in "Rosemaling Rogaland Style" was published. In 1979, "Intermediate Rosemaling, Rogaland Style" was published, in 1982 "Telemark and Rogaland" and in 1984 "Collection of Designs" which covered more advanced type of painting and new techniques.

I did travel, teaching for about five years all over the United States and Canada. I enjoyed this very much and it was really the beginning of the Rogaland style of painting that is so widely known all over the U.S.

In February, 1986, I received the Community Appreciation Award from the Stoughton High School Norwegian Dancers which I value very much.

At present time, I am teaching in my studio and I plan on several seminars for the summer of 1986. Also, I'm teaching for the Rosemaling Association.

I would like to do more painting and designing this year and take time to enjoy some of the training I've had. Something new and different has always come out of reviewing all I've learned before. I love to do new designs so that others may use them and we can continue to learn and perpetuate rosemaling in this country.

Awarded Gold Medal 1970

Vi Thode

Anno 1986

ViThode

ViThode

ViThode

Margaret Mary (Miller) Utzinger

Los Altos Hills, CA

I was born in Sturgeon Bay, Wisconsin in 1935 and received my Bachelor's Degree in Science in Home Economics and Retailing at the University of Wisconsin at Madison in 1957. My interest in Rosemaling came as a natural result of my Norwegian heritage. My mother was totally Norwegian and my father was German and Norwegian, so our home was Norwegian and decorated by my mother with this distinctive type of painting.

My training in Rosemaling, however, began under my father's guidance some years after my mother's death. By that time he had become a nationally recognized painter of watercolor and egg tempera but he admired this type of folk art, and was glad to have me take an interest in it. But my professional training in it started in 1969 in Decorah, Iowa, when the Norwegian-American Museum first offered classes in Rosemaling under Norwegian Master Rosemalers. I continued studying there for some years under Sigmund Aarseth and Nils Ellingard and also traveled to Norway on the first rosemaling tour sponsored by the Museum. All this preceeded my marriage to William Utzinger, a surgeon affiliated with Stanford University Hospital in Palo Alto, California.

My professional work in Rosemaling has been mostly in three different areas, painting, teaching and writing. The painting has been done in private homes in Wisconsin and in the San Francisco Bay area of California. I also worked on three different DECORATOR SHOW HOUSES in the Bay area, in a Ski Lodge in Squaw Valley and in stores in Los Altos and in Sturgeon Bay. The teaching was done in Wisconsin in Summer classes over a 10-year period and in Los Altos in year round classes for 15 years.

The style of my painting is probably most closely related to that of the Telemark area in Norway. It shows some influence of my mentor Sigmund Aarseth and is rather free flowing, colorful and feminine. I feel that it adds informality, warmth and charm to interiors that might otherwise be rather impersonal and sterile.

But probably my most important accomplishment in the field of Rosemaling is the co-authoring with Sigmund Aarseth of a comprehensive and definitive book titled NORWEGIAN ROSEMALING—DECORATIVE PAINTING ON WOOD. Scribners published it in 1974 and it has been on the market in hard cover for 12 years and in paperback for the last two years.

M. M. Utzinger

Margaret Miller Utzinger

Margaret Miller Utzinger

Pat Virch

I was encouraged, in my youth, to illustrate flowers and scenes around me using charcoal, watercolors and pastels. Art was a favorite subject in school and I continued to paint for the joy it gave me. My earliest decorative paintings were done on the toys Niron and I made for our children. My first rosemaling teacher was Violet Christopherson in 1962. Our family moved from Wisconsin to Michigan in 1963. I had to continue rosemaling without a teacher. Our family vacations were often trips in the Midwest and East Coast states researching folk arts, with the emphasis on Norwegian rosemaling as we both come from Norwegian families.

I furthered my studies with Norwegian rosemalers at the Norwegian-American Museum, however the greatest influence on my style of painting has been the paintings of the 18th and 19th century rosemalers we have seen while researching in Norway these past 15 years. I have participated in every National Rosemaling Exhibition sponsored by the N-A Museum since 1967 and was awarded the Gold Medal of Honor in 1974.

My teaching career began in 1964 in my studio and in Adult Ed. and was confined to Michigan until 1972 when I started to Travel Teach. I have conducted workshops/seminars/lectures in most of the United States also in Canada, Netherlands, Norway, and Switzerland. I have been a member of the National Society of Tole and Decorative Painters since its origin in 1972 and have taught classes at every annual convention.

The first published article I wrote was for CREATIVE CRAFTS MAG. in 1968 and I have gone on to write four books about rosemaling, TRADITIONAL NORWEGIAN ROSEMALING 1970, ROSEMALING IN THE ROUND 1976, TELEMARK TECHNIQUES 1979, and NORWEGIAN ROSEMALING—FOLK ART FUN in 1983. My research in the American folk arts led to the writing of DECORATED TINWARE—AN EARLY AMERICAN FOLK ART in 1977. In 1981 I wrote SWEDISH FOLK PAINTING OF DALARNA. In 1972-73 I produced two portfolios of colored prints, and have further designed more than 55 pattern pages and a total of 36 different colored prints. Since 1967 we have circulated our WOOD AND TIN DECORATOR'S SUPPLY CATALOG with unusual wood items and painting supplies all over the USA, Canada and 12 foreign countries.

My work in rosemaling has been feature stories in the following magazines, Norwegian ALLERS 1971, VIKING 1973, DECORATING AND CRAFTS IDEAS 1980 and LOG HOME DECOR 1985. Newspapers writing about our work include NEW YORK TIMES 1973, MILWAUKEE JOURNAL 1981, GREEN BAY PRESS GAZETTE 1976 and others. My painted wood projects and instructions have been in DECORATING AND CRAFTS IDEAS April and October 1980, Sept 81, March 82; cover story June 1975 AMERICAN HOME MAGAZINE; AMERICAN HOME CRAFTS 1975; COUNTRY LIVING May 1985. My decorated tinware was shown on the cover of McCALLS NEEDLEWORK AND CRAFTS 1979 and 1985. Other magazine articles were CRAFTS 'N THINGS, CRAFTS, DECORATIVE PAINTER, TOLE WORLD and numerous hobby trade magazines. My work and instructions are included in the Time-Life series FAMILY CREATIVE CRAFTS WORKSHOP ENCYCLOPEDIA, Vol. 15, 1976.

Together Niron and I have built and decorated our charming "Folk Art Cottage VINJEBU" in the Michigan northwoods. We share this retreat with my summer seminar students. The doors are painted with rosemaling, walls and ceilings are filled with flowing acanthus scrolls and scenes of Scandinavia. The outside of the cabin is decorated in the Bavarian manner.

Since 1980 we have been sharing Scandinavia and Central European crafts with others on our FOLK ART ADVENTURE TOURS. We visit Norway, Sweden, Finland, Denmark, Germany, Austria, Switzerland, Luxemburg, Belgium and The Netherlands to see the finest collections and introduce them to the craftsmen who are keeping these old handcrafts alive.

My most challenging work had to have been the rosemaling of the ceiling of a Norwegian sod roof home built by the actor Ben Blue in 1936, now restored by the present owners. From this huge project to the painting of miniature dollhouse furniture makes me aware of how flexible a decorative painter must have to be.

It has been a most satisfying and fulfilling 30 some years I have spent in this wonderful world of folk painting. Teaching, sharing and painting has made my life very exciting and full of purpose, and I want to be able to continue this work for many years. Here is our family motto, "Those who bring sunshine into the lives of others, cannot keep it from themselves." Thank you for allowing me this opportunity to share even further and please accept all this remembering that "FOLK ARTS ARE FUN."

Awarded Gold Medal 1974

Pat Virch '86

Pat Virch
'86

Trudy Sondrol Wasson

Eden Prairie, MN

A trip to Norway was taken in 1971 to meet many of my relatives. Many relatives had rosemaling in their homes. I decided it would be interesting to learn enough about rosemaling to paint a few pieces for my children.

In 1973, I found out about classes at Vesterheim, the Norwegian-American Museum in Decorah, Iowa. The first class I attended was taught by Nils Ellingsgard from Hallingdal. By the end of the class, I was "hooked"! Since my first class, I have spent more than 50 weeks studying with Nils, Bergljot Lunde from Sand in Rogaland, Sigmund Aarseth, Aanund Lunden, Knut Andersen, Ruth Nordbo, Gunnar Bo, Olav Tveiten, as well as Hans Prinz from Dalarna, Sweden, and several American teachers. These seminars have given me an outstanding background in all the major styles of rosemaling as well as several of the lesser known styles.

I entered my first competition in 1974, the National Rosemaling Exhibition, held during Nordic Fest in Decorah. In 1975, I entered a tilt top table which won a blue ribbon and a trunk which won a red ribbon. The tilt top table became part of an exhibit of "Rosemaling in America" which toured Norway and was on display in many of their museums. It is now part of the permanent collection at Vesterheim. In 1976, I won a red ribbon on a bowl and a white ribbon on a flat bread box, giving me the necessary points to receive my Medal of Honor. By that time, I had been rosemaling for only three years.

In August, 1981, I traveled to Norway and spent a month studying and researching the old rosemaling and the artists. I had the opportunity to study numerous pieces at Bygdoy in Oslo, Glomdalsmuseet in Elverum, Maihaugen in Lillehammer, Valdres Museum in Fagernes, Aal and Nesbyen Museums in Hallingdal, Voss Museum, Bergen Museum, Hordaland Museum in Stend, Rogaland Folk Museum near Sand, Lolandsbua near Sand, Stavanger Museum, as well as the museums in Skien and Drammen. I was fortunate to be invited into so many homes in several of the areas to study and photograph more old pieces of rosemaling. The extensive research I have done has been an extremely interesting part of my study of rosemaling.

In 1983, I wrote and published my first book, OLD ROGALAND ROSEMALING. This book is based on my research in the Rogaland area in 1981. The designs are inspired from the old rosemaling I had studied. Since I want authenticity in my rosemaling, I had numerous requests to publish a book demonstrating the method used in Norway to paint Rogaland style rosemaling. In 1984, I wrote and published AUTHENTIC NORWEGIAN ROSEMALING, ROGALAND STYLE, VOLUME I. Both books are available in the United States and in Norway. It was a personal goal to write books which would be respected by the Norwegians and distributed in Norway, also.

I have published four design sets. Sets three and four are still available. I have recently published several design packets including trunk designs, fabric painting, and other miscellaneous wood pieces. I will have at least 25 packets available by May 1.

I am of Norwegian descent. My father is from Vang in Valdres and I still have many relatives in the area. I recently completed another week of study on the rosemaling in the Valdres area with Nils Ellingsgard. My mother's family is from eastern Norway near Sweden.

I teach seminars all over the United States several weeks a year. I have judged at least one competition a year and have served as a judge for the National Rosemaling Exhibit sponsored by Vesterheim.

My goal in rosemaling is to continue to study and research and pass it on to my students. Rosemaling is the art of my ancestors and I want to preserve the authenticity of it.

I now reside in Eden Prairie, Minnesota, with my husband and son, Thomas. We also have three adult children, Julie, Mark, and Eric.

I am a Life Member of Vesterheim and teach there at least one week every year. I also hold memberships in numerous art organizations.

Awarded Gold Medal 1976

Recipes

1985 Trudy Sondrol Wasson

1985 Trudy Søndrol Wasson